HAVE FUN READING THIS BOOK!

IT OFFERS SOME REAL SURVIVAL TIPS. BUT THE SETTINGS ARE NOT REAL. THINK ABOUT HOW YOU CAN USE THESE HACKS IN REAL LIFE. USE COMMON SENSE. BE SAFE AND ASK AN ADULT FOR PERMISSION AND HELP WHEN NEEDED.

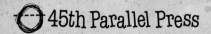
45th Parallel Press

Published in the United States of America by Cherry Lake Publishing
Ann Arbor, Michigan
www.cherrylakepublishing.com

Reading Adviser: Marla Conn, MS, Ed., Literacy specialist, Read-Ability, Inc.
Book Designer: Felicia Macheske

Photo Credits: © tulpahn/Shutterstock.com, cover; © Phonlamai Photo/Shutterstock.com, 5; © Gorodenkoff/
Shutterstock.com, 6; © Ranta Images/Shutterstock.com, 9; © Tatiana Popova/Shutterstock.com, 13; © Samuel
Borges Photography/Shutterstock.com, 14; © Mega Pixel/Shutterstock.com, 14; © AVS-Images/Shutterstock.
com, 17; © Seeme/Shutterstock.com, 19; © Roman Samokhin/Shutterstock.com, 21; © TAVEESUK/
Shutterstock.com, 22; © Madlen/Shutterstock.com, 23; © Konstantin Remizov/Shutterstock.com, 25; © IM_
VISUALS/Shutterstock.com, 27; © adempercem/Shutterstock.com, 29

Other Images Throughout: © SrsPvl Witch/Shutterstock.com; © Igor Vitkovskiy/Shutterstock.com; © FabrikaSimf/
Shutterstock.com; © bulbspark/Shutterstock.com; © donatas1205/Shutterstock.com; © NinaM/Shutterstock.com;
© Picsfive/Shutterstock.com; © prapann/Shutterstock.com; © S_Kuzmin/Shutterstock.com © autsawin uttisin/
Shutterstock.com; © xpixel/Shutterstock.com; © OoddySmile/Shutterstock.com; © ilikestudio/Shutterstock.com;
© Kues/Shutterstock.com; © bioraven/Shutterstock.com; © bioraven/Shutterstock.com, © jehsomwang/
Shutterstock.com; © ankomando/Shutterstock.com; © A-spring/Shutterstock.com; © Edvard Molnar/
Shutterstock.com

45th Parallel Press is an imprint of Cherry Lake Publishing.

Library of Congress Cataloging-in-Publication Data

Names: Loh-Hagan, Virginia, author.
Title: AI uprising hacks / by Virginia Loh-Hagan.
Other titles: Artificial intelligence uprising hacks
Description: Ann Arbor, MI : Cherry Lake Publishing, [2019] | Series: Could
 you survive? | Includes bibliographical
 references and index.
Identifiers: LCCN 2019003647| ISBN 9781534147829 (hardcover) | ISBN
 9781534150683 (pbk.) | ISBN 9781534149250 (pdf) | ISBN 9781534152113
(hosted ebook)
Subjects: LCSH: Survival—Juvenile literature. | Artificial
 intelligence—Juvenile literature. | Technological innovations—Juvenile literature.
Classification: LCC GF86 .L64 2019 | DDC 613.6/9—dc23
LC record available at https://lccn.loc.gov/2019003647

Cherry Lake Publishing would like to acknowledge the work of The Partnership for 21st Century Skills.
Please visit *www.p21.org* for more information.

Printed in the United States of America
Corporate Graphics

Dr. Virginia Loh-Hagan is an author, university professor, former classroom teacher, and curriculum
designer. She has a lot of tech devices in her house. She lives in San Diego with her very tall husband
and very naughty dogs. To learn more about her, visit www.virginialoh.com.

COULD YOU SURVIVE
AN AI
UPRISING?

THIS BOOK COULD SAVE YOUR LIFE!

AI stands for **artificial intelligence**. Artificial means fake. It means not human. Intelligence means the ability to think. Artificial intelligence refers to computer systems. Examples are robots and machines. These robots and machines can learn and think. They're smart. They're designed to copy humans. They handle tasks in an intelligent way.

An uprising is an act of rising up. It's a takeover. An **AI uprising** is when robots and machines take over control. AI assumes power over humans.

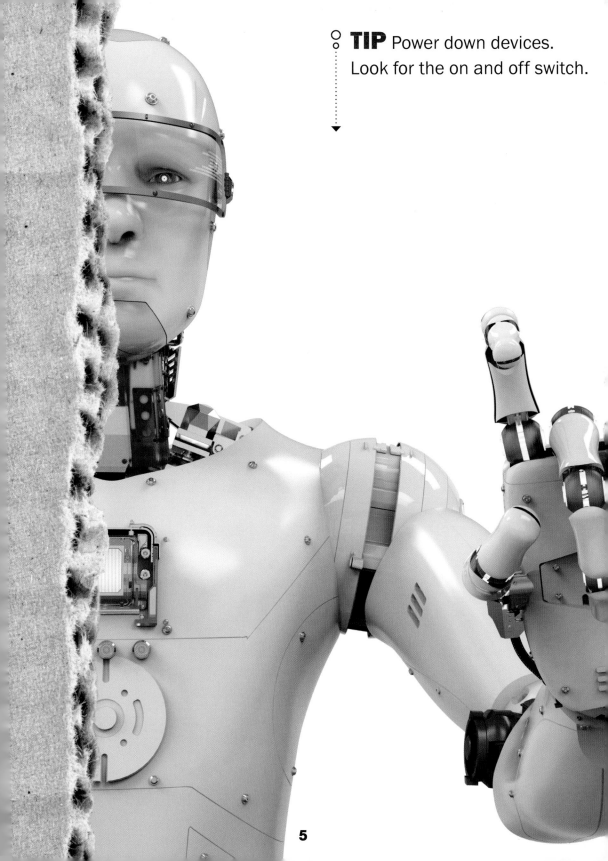

○ **TIP** Power down devices.
Look for the on and off switch.

We use technology for everything. Technology is all around us. Right now, we tell technology what to do. Right now, we're smarter than technology. But new technology is always being created. AI is growing smarter every day. It works faster than us. It knows more. It can store more information. One day, AI might be smarter than us. One day, AI might be telling us what to do.

Some people are really worried about an AI uprising. They think AI will take away our jobs. They think AI wants to turn humans into slaves. They think AI wants to kill humans.

TIP Gather a team of hackers. These are people who can break into computer systems.

Scientists think AI will be able to do all the things humans can do by 2060. At that time, humans may be **terminated**. Terminated means no longer existing. But you might be one of the lucky survivors. To live, you have to be smart. First, stop using technology. Second, get off the **grid**. A grid is a network of power sources. It connects technology. You'll have to survive without technology.

Most importantly, know how to survive. Keep this in mind:

- You can only live 3 minutes without air.

- You can only live 3 days without water.

- You can only live 3 weeks without food.

This book offers you survival **hacks**, or tricks. Always be prepared. Good luck to you.

TIP Turn off
your screens.

SCIENCE CONNECTION

Computers can solve problems. How do they do it? First, AI collects facts. It does this when humans input information. Input means to enter. Humans code. They program. They do internet searches. This all gives AI information. AI can also collect information from sensors. Some AI may have special tools. Cameras can see things. Devices can hear things. Second, AI compares the information to stored data. Stored data is information stored in its system. AI connects information. It runs through different possible actions. It predicts the best actions. Most computers can only solve problems they're programmed to solve. An example is chess programs. But AI is special. AI has the ability to learn. It tries things out. It remembers things. It copies human actions. It stores all information. It uses this information in the future. It does things automatically. AI is always changing and growing. Scientists guess how and why humans learn. They test ideas using robots.

CHAPTER 1

HIDE IN A FARADAY CAGE!

Get away from technology. AI controls you through machines. Escape to a **remote** place. Remote means far away from cities. But take important devices. Examples are radios and phones. You'll need to create a Faraday cage to put them in. These cages block out electric charges.

HACK

1. Get a steel trash can and lid.

2. Line the inside with foil. Add at least 3 layers. Make sure there aren't any holes or rips. This is extra protection.

3. Add a layer of cardboard. Do this to the lid as well.

4. Cover the cardboard with plastic wrap or bag.

5. Wrap the devices in cloth. Put them in a plastic bag. This will also stop water damage.

6. Put the devices in the can. Cover the can with the lid.

TIP Put foil on your windows and walls.

The key to this hack is **conduction**.

Conduction is a process. It's the movement of electricity through an object. Faraday cages have 2 layers. The outside layer is electrically conductive. This means electric waves can move on it. These waves are spread out. The inside layer is nonconductive. This means that electric waves can't move inside. Electric charges are canceled out. We're surrounded by invisible electric waves. Too much electricity can **electrocute** us. Electrocute means to harm or kill with an electric shock. A Faraday cage is a hollow conductor. Charges remain on the outside. What's inside is protected.

TIP Make sure you have batteries for your devices.

CHAPTER 2

SEE THE LIGHT!

AI controls electric power. In an uprising, AI will most likely turn off the lights. This scares people. Prepare to live in complete darkness. Learn how to make your own oil lamp.

HACK

1. Find canned fish. Get the ones packed in oil.

2. Eat the fish. Save the oil in the can.

3. Get a string mop. Take out one of the threads. This will be the **wick**. A wick is the part of the lamp that burns.

4. Soak the thread in the oil. Leave it in the can. Leave a part outside the can.

5. Light the end outside the can. This will burn for many hours. Move around as needed.

TIP Collect as many canned goods as you can.

explained by STEM

The key to this hack is the wick.

Wicks are a bundle of **fibers**. Fibers are small threads.

Wicks use **capillary** action. A capillary is a vessel. Capillary action is the movement of **liquid**. Liquid is water form. In oil lamps, the liquid is the oil. The oil moves into the spaces of a **porous** object. Porous means having holes. Wicks are porous. They use the forces of **adhesion** to draw the oil. Adhesion means stickiness. Wicks move the oil from the can to the fire. The oil keeps wicks from burning up. Flames burn just above the wicks' surface.

Oil lamps have been used for hundreds of years. They make more light than candles.

TIP Trim wicks to stop smoke.

REAL-LIFE CONNECTION

Go is an ancient board game. It's 2,500 years old. It's harder than chess. It has many possible moves. It's hard to predict. No computer had ever beaten a human until 2015. Fan Hui is a Chinese-born Frenchman. He's a champion Go player. He's won many contests. He competed against an AI program. The AI program was made by Google. It is called AlphaGo. It beat Hui. This was the first time an AI beat a human professional player. Hui said, "I know AlphaGo is a computer. But if no one told me, maybe I would think the player was a little strange, but a very strong player, a real person." In 2016, AlphaGo competed against Lee Sedol. Sedol is a South Korean Go player. He's a champion as well. He played 5 games against AlphaGo. AlphaGo won 4 of the 5 games. Sedol said, "I failed ... I wanted it to end well."

CHAPTER 3

MAKE A FIRE!

Living away from technology means you need to be resourceful. You'll need to make a fire. A fire will keep you warm. It'll let you cook. It'll give you more light.

TIP Put dryer lint in a toilet paper roll. This can be used as fuel for your fire.

HACK

1. Make a fire pit. Put wood and **tinder** in the center. Tinder is needed to start fires. Examples are twigs or leaves.

2. Get a soda can.

3. Rub chocolate at the bottom of the can. (If you don't have chocolate, use toothpaste.) Add more chocolate as needed. Rub for 30 minutes.

4. Wash off with water. This makes a shiny surface.

5. Point the bottom of the can toward the sun.

6. Create a focused ray of light.

7. Aim the light directly at the tinder. Do this from about an inch away.

TIP Use mirrors and lenses to start fires.

STEM

The key to this hack is the soda can.

A regular can has fine lines. It doesn't reflect well. It scatters the sun's rays. This means the light can't form a single point.

The chocolate acts like a **polish**. A polish is an **abrasive**. Abrasives remove surface defects. They remove a thin layer. They make surfaces smooth. Rubbing the chocolate on the can makes it shiny. It turns it into a **parabolic** mirror. Parabolic means U-shaped. A parabolic mirror is a good reflector. It reflects sunlight. It focuses the light. It shines the light onto a small area. It heats up the area. It makes a flame.

CHAPTER 4

GROW A GARDEN!

AI doesn't need to eat food.
But you do. Make your own food.
Plant your own garden.

TIP Grow garlic. It improves the taste
of food. It can be a medicine.

HACK

1. Get a dozen eggs. Use a thumbtack. Prick a hole in the bottom of each egg.

2. Remove the top 1/3 of each eggshell. Use a small knife. Gently pick away.

3. Empty the raw eggs. Make into a meal.

4. Wash and boil the eggshells. Kill the germs.

5. Dry the eggshells. Put the eggshells back in the carton.

6. Spoon soil into each eggshell. Plant some seeds.

7. Place in sunlight. Add water. Watch the seeds sprout.

8. Move the sprouts to a garden. Squeeze the eggshells to crush them a little bit. Plant the eggshells with the sprouts.

explained by

STEM

The key to this hack is the eggshells.

Eggshells are the hard outer covering of eggs. They have a thin skin attached to the inside. They're made of healthy things. They're mostly calcium. They also have protein and other minerals. They rot when planted. They make the soil richer. This helps plants grow.

Eggshells are bumpy. They have up to 17,000 tiny holes. Air and water pass through. Eggshells also have a thin coating. This coating keeps out germs and dust. Eggshells are great plant pots.

Growing seeds in eggshells is good for plants. Sprouted seeds are stronger when planted.

TIP Compost your leftovers. This helps the soil. It recycles your waste.

SPOTLIGHT BIOGRAPHY

Sophia is a robot. She was activated in 2016. She looks like a human. She acts like a human. She was modeled after Audrey Hepburn. Hepburn was a famous actress. Sophia is able to make over 50 expressions on her face. She makes human motions. She can answer questions. She can have simple talks about certain topics. She can make jokes. She has feelings. In 2017, she became the first robot to become a citizen. She became a Saudi Arabian citizen. She was given a United Nations title. She was the first nonhuman to do so. She uses AI. She has cameras in her eyes. She can process speech. She has legs that can walk. She was created by David Hanson. Hanson used to work at Disney. He said, "Our robots will eventually evolve to become super intelligent genius machines that can help us solve the most challenging problems we face here in the world."

CHAPTER 5

CALL A FRIEND!

It's best to avoid technology during an AI uprising. But you should stay in contact with people. You need to make plans to defeat robots. Make a walkie-talkie from tin cans.

TIP Don't trust what you hear on devices. The information may be false. Do your own research.

HACK

1. Get 2 tin cans. Remove the lids. Clean them.

2. Get a long piece of string.

3. Turn both cans upside down.

4. Use a nail and hammer. Make a hole in the bottom of each can.

5. Put one end of the string through the hole of one of the cans. Tie a knot inside the can.

6. Repeat with the other can.

7. Hold one can to your mouth. Talk into it.

8. Have a friend hold the other can to their ear.

TIP Form or join a good team. You can't win a war by yourself.

STEM

The key to this hack is **vibrations**.

Vibrations are sound waves. They're movements that go up and down. They travel through different materials.

Our voices cause vibrations. They usually travel through the air. But in this hack, they travel through the string. Our voices move down the string instead of air. The string needs to be stretched tight. But don't make it too tight.

This hack is similar to how guitars work. Strings are plucked. They vibrate. The vibrations move. They go to the body. The body serves as an **amplifier**. Amplifiers make vibrations loud enough to be heard.

DID YOU KNOW?

- Many people shop online. AI is keeping track. Computers study shopping habits. They learn about shoppers. They study what shoppers buy. They study how shoppers buy. They predict what shoppers will buy next. They recommend products. They give deals. In the future, AI may make shopping lists for shoppers. They may order things for shoppers.

- Japanese and French companies made a robot called Pepper. They did this in 2014. Pepper interacts with humans. It works in customer service. It greets people. It works in people's homes. It can read emotions. It analyzes expressions. It analyzes voice tones. Its main job is to "make people happy."

- Elon Musk is a famous innovator and businessman. He's always coming up with tech ideas. He's worried about AI's effect on humans. He founded Neuralink in 2016. Neuralink creates tech tools. It studies the link between human brains and computers. Musk was inspired by reading science-fiction books by Iain M. Banks.

- Eugene Goostman is a chatbot. A chatbot is a type of AI. It's programmed to talk. Eugene sounds like a teenage boy. He passed the Turing test in 2014. The test states that if a computer can be mistaken for a human, then it's intelligent. Eugene was entered in a contest. About 33 percent of judges thought Goostman was a real human.

- John McCarthy was a professor. He worked at Stanford University. He taught computer science. He created the term *artificial intelligence*.

CONSIDER THIS!

TAKE A POSITION!

What is scarier: an alien invasion or an AI uprising? Argue your point with reasons and evidence.

SAY WHAT?

Technology has changed how we live. It has made our lives easier. But it does have its downsides. Explain how technology is good. Explain how it's bad.

THINK ABOUT IT!

Are you interested in coding? People are needed to program computers. Computer science is a growing field. Everything is run by computers. Coding is a valuable skill. There are more male coders than female coders. Why do you think this is? Girls Who Code is an organization. It's the largest U.S. group for girls that offers computer training programs. Why do we need more female coders?

LEARN MORE!

Doeden, Matt. *Can You Survive an Artificial Intelligence Uprising?* North Mankato, MN: Capstone Press, 2016.

Robot. New York, NY: DK Children's, 2018.

Smibert, Angie, and Alexis Cornell (illust.). *Artificial Intelligence: Thinking Machines and Smart Robots with Science Activities for Kids.* White River Junction, VT: Nomad Press, 2018.

GLOSSARY

abrasive (uh-BRAY-siv) a substance used to remove surface defects to make an object smoother

adhesion (ad-HEE-zhuhn) the process of sticking

AI uprising (AY-EYE UHP-rye-zing) a takeover of the human race by smart robots and machines

amplifier (AM-pluh-fye-ur) something that makes sound louder

artificial intelligence (ahr-tuh-FISH-uhl in-TEL-ih-juhns) computer systems (robots and machines) that can think and learn like a human

capillary (KAP-uh-ler-ee) a vessel that moves a substance from one area to another

conduction (kuhn-DUHKT-shuhn) the process by which heat or electricity is directly transmitted through a substance

electrocute (ih-LEK-truh-kyoot) to hurt or kill by an electric shock

fibers (FYE-burz) small threads twisted together to form a cord

grid (GRID) a network of power sources, how all technology is connected

hacks (HAKS) tricks

liquid (LIK-wid) water form

parabolic (par-uh-BAH-lik) U-shaped

polish (PAH-lish) a substance that smoothes out a surface

porous (POR-uhs) having small holes through which liquid or air can pass

remote (rih-MOHT) a faraway location away from people and cities

terminated (TUR-muh-nate-id) to no longer be existing, to be ended, to be killed

tinder (TIN-dur) things needed to start a fire, like twigs or leaves

vibrations (vye-BRAY-shuhnz) sound waves

wick (WIK) a strip of porous material that draws liquid fuel to the flame

INDEX